Hi. My name is Emily Elizabeth. My Big Red Dog, Clifford, and I are looking for things that start with the letter a. The word apple starts with the letter a. **Circle all the pictures that start with the letter a.**

egg   arrow   apple

toy   ant   ball   acorn

B b

T-Bone likes to play with a ball. The word ball starts with a b. Everything on this page starts with the letter b. **Write the first letter of each word.**

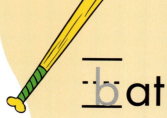
bat

_alloon

_all

_ird

_ee

Draw something else that starts with the letter b here.

Clifford's and Cleo's names both start with the letter C. **Find the thing in each row that does not start with the letter c. Mark an X on it.**

cat   cow   dog

hat   carrot   cone

  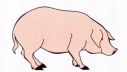

cup   car   pig

Draw something else that starts with the letter c here.

Clifford's abc

Dd

Clifford is a dog. The word dog starts with the letter d. **Connect the dots to find something else that starts with the letter d.**

drum   esk   og

These things also start with the letter d. Colour them.

Clifford Ages 3-5

My name is Emily Elizabeth. Both of my names start with the letter E. The words eagle, eggs, and eight also start with the letter e.

Help me follow the road that leads to the eagle's eggs.

Ee

eight eagle eggs

Write how many eggs are in the nest:

eggs

Ff

T-Bone is looking at a fish. The word fish starts with the letter f. **Draw lines between the fish that are the same.**

frog   ox

These things also start with the letter f. Colour them.

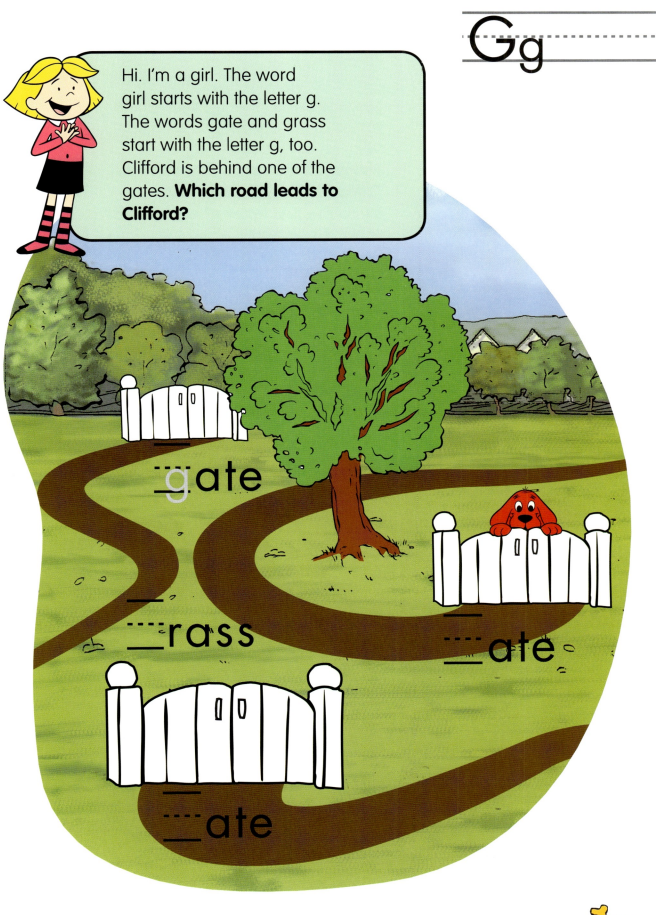

T-Bone and Cleo really like ice-cream! They also like lemonade with ice-cubes. The word ice starts with the letter i.
Colour the ice-cream cone.
Fill in the missing letters.

__i__ce-cream

____ce-cube

Draw your own ice-cream cone here.

Clifford's abc

Jj

I'm going to decorate my old jacket.
The word jacket starts with the letter j.
Can you help me make it look good?
Draw lots of funny buttons and other things on my jacket.

__ar   __umbo __et   __am

These things also start with the letter j.

Clifford Ages 3–5

T-Bone is dreaming that he can fly like a kite. The word kite starts with the letter k. Let's find some other things that start with k.
Colour the kites with k words.

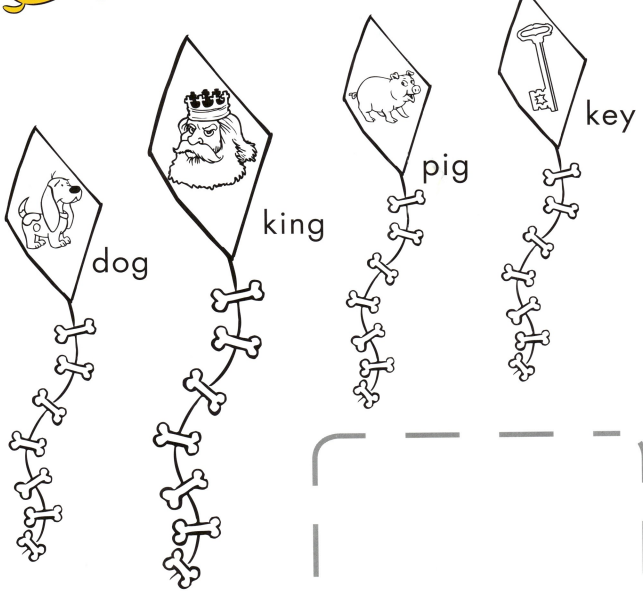

dog

king

pig

key

Draw something else that starts with the letter k here.

Ll

Cleo is trying to reach the ladder. The word ladder starts with the letter l. **Follow the road that will take Cleo to the ladder. What is at the top of the ladder?**

lunch box

ladder

_eaf

_og

There are 4 monkeys and 4 mice hiding on this page. The words monkey and mice start with the letter m.

Can you help me to find and circle them?

mice   onkey

Clifford's abc

Nn

Clifford has found a number written in the sand. The word number starts with the letter n. **Can you help Clifford connect the dots? What number is in the sand?**

n̲ine

The word nest also starts with the letter n. **Draw a nest here.**

n̲est

Clifford and I like to play by the ocean. The word ocean starts with the letter o.
Draw circles around the other things on this page that start with the letter o. Write the first letter of each word below.

ocean

  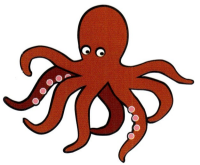

___ar ___range ___ctopus

Pp

I'm doing a puzzle. The word puzzle starts with the letter p. **Help me finish my puzzle. Draw a line from each piece to the place where it belongs.**

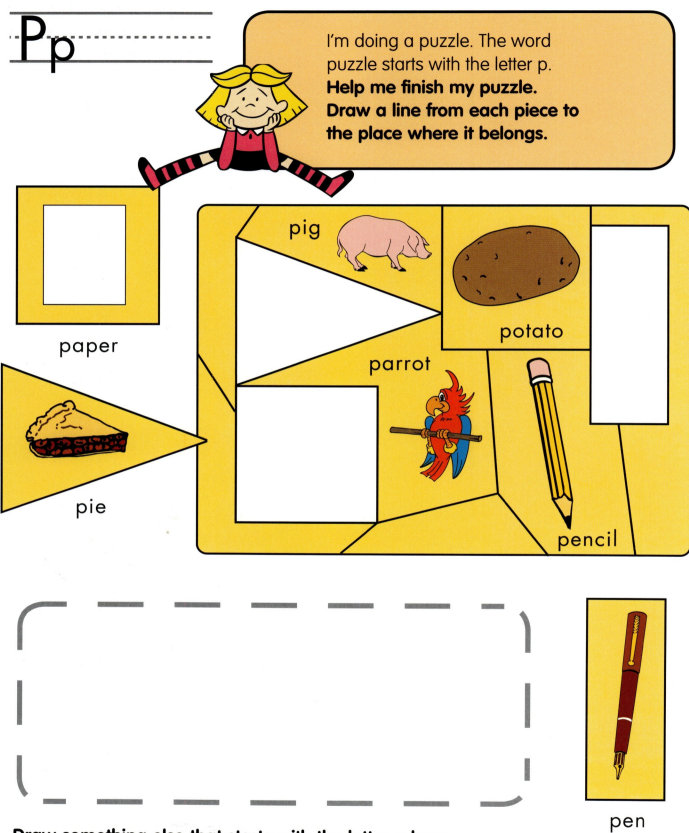

paper

pie

pig

potato

parrot

pencil

pen

Draw something else that starts with the letter p here.

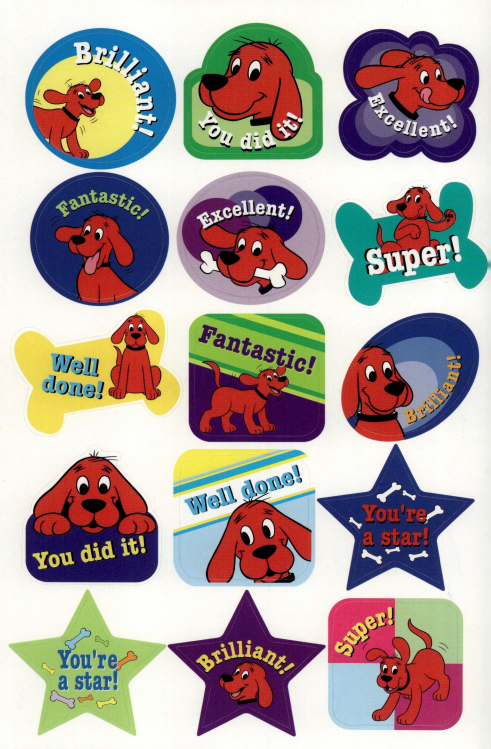

Shhh. BE QUIET! T-Bone wants to have a sleep on that quilt! The words quilt and QUIET start with q.

How many capital Q's do you see? How many lower case q's do you see?

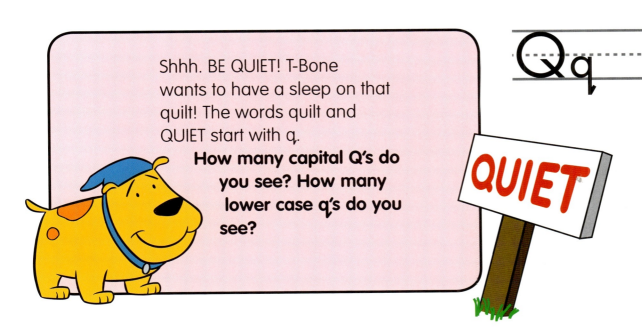

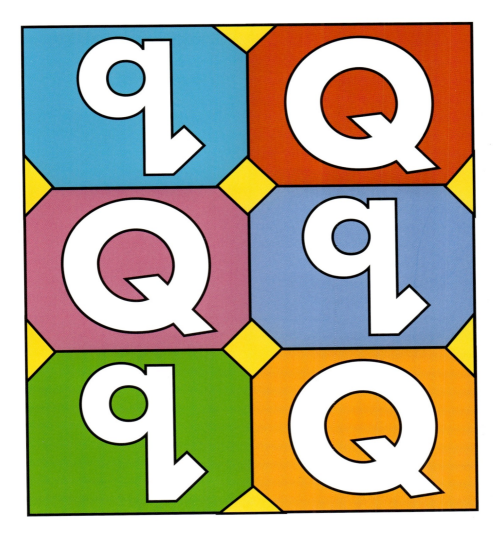

quilt

Clifford's abc

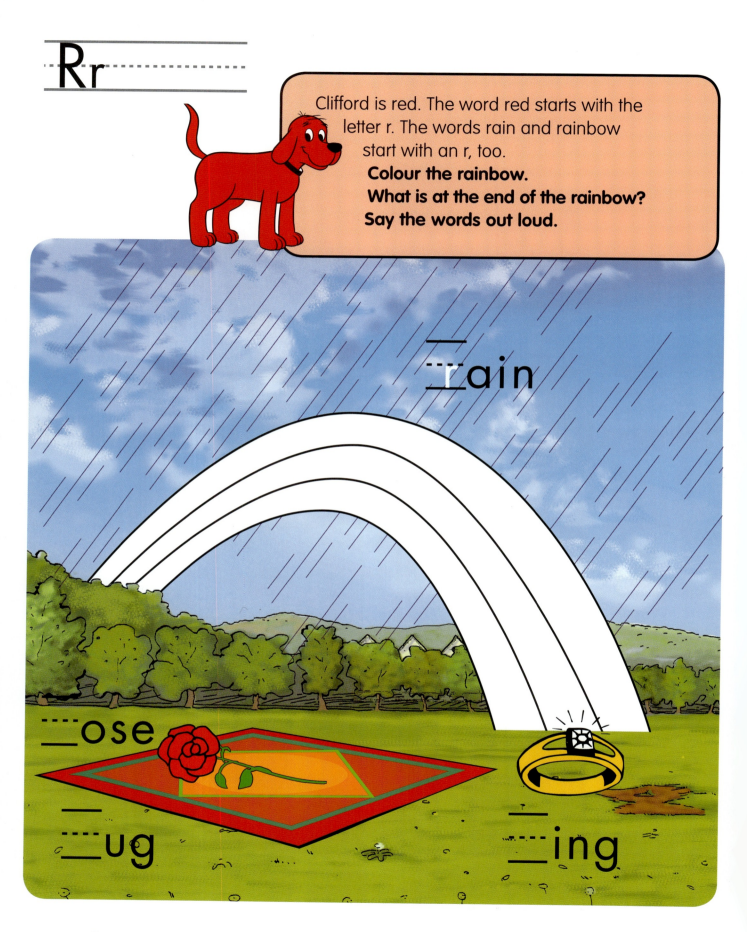

Ss

Hey! Let's sort socks! I can see 6 socks on this page. Can you? The words six and socks start with the letter s.
Draw lines between the socks that are the same.

_un

The word sun also starts with the letter s. Draw a sun here.

socks

Clifford's abc

Tt

T-Bone's name starts with the letter T. So does the word toy! Can you help us put our toys away?

Draw lines from the things that start with t to the toy box.

top

tortoise

tiger

bone

bucket

ball

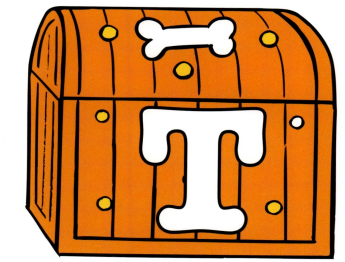

It's raining. I need to put something up to keep me dry. The word up starts with the letter u.

Connect the dots to see what I need. It starts with the letter u, too. Colour it.

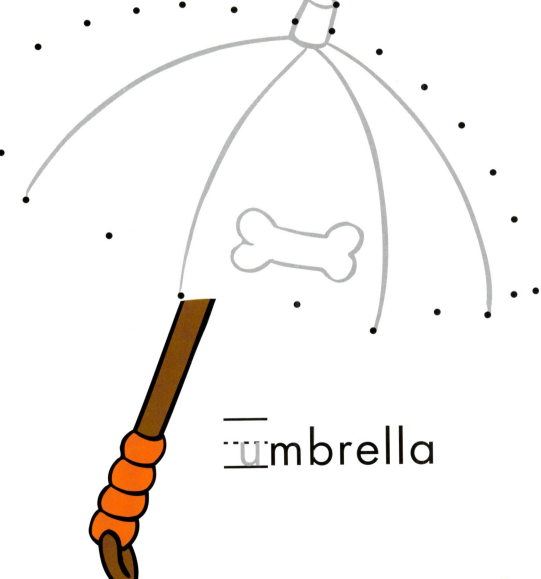

umbrella

Cleo and T-Bone are near the water. They are watching the waves. The word water starts with the letter w. So does the word wave.
Circle all the other things that start with w. Write the first letter of each word.

_orm

_and   shell

_eb

bone   _atch

Clifford's abc

Look at all these X-rays! X-ray starts with the letter X.

Mark an X on the X-ray in each row that is not like the others.

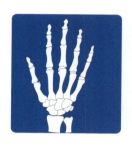  

  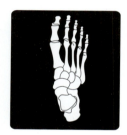

 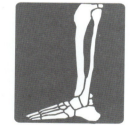 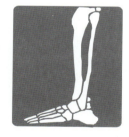

Clifford Ages 3-5

Clifford is looking for yellow yo-yos in his garden. The words yellow and yo-yo start with the letter y.
Circle all the yellow yo-yos.

ellow   yo-yo

Zz

T-Bone is playing peepo with an animal in the zoo. The name of the animal starts with the letter z. So does the word zoo.

Connect the dots to see T-Bone's new friend.

zebra

Cleo and T-Bone are looking at numbers.
Trace the first letters of the number words. Then colour all the numbers.

1 2 3 4 5
one two three four five

6 7 8 9 10
six seven eight nine ten

Clifford's abc

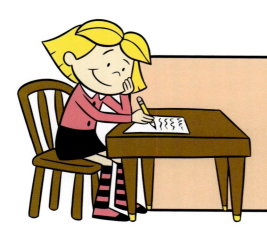

Let's match colours.
Draw lines between the colours and their matching colour words. Trace the letters of each colour word.

green

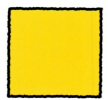

blue

red

yellow

Cleo's and Clifford's names start with the letter C. T-Bone's name starts with the letter T. My name starts with the letter E. What does your name start with?

Write the letter

Draw something that starts with the same letter here.

Write your name here

Look what Clifford has found. **Draw lines between the things that start with the same letter.** Trace the first letter of each word.

apple

cap

cup

boot

bone

arrow

Let's trace all the letters of the alphabet.

a b c d e f g
h i j k l m n
o p q r s t u
v w x y z

Clifford's abc